King William IV, newly ascended to the throne but not yet crowned, lost no time in visiting Brighton. His brother's favourite domain of 40,000 people would be his. And kindly old sea salt that he was, he pressed Mrs Fitzherbert to visit him at The Royal Pavilion. When told that ill-health prevented her, he sought her out in her own house in The Steine.

The old woman, seventy-four years of age now, happy at last to be so decently treated, was thus to become a regular visitor to The Pavilion. Ought she to have been queen? Had she really been married to George IV? Certainly she stood by her story; she even showed the King her marriage certificate.

But what good were marriage certificates, she must have reflected. Why, there were others in the same boat. Even in Brighton at about this time there were at least two other women with marriage certificates and both of them married to the same man. What good did their certificates do them?

Did a marriage certificate save Celia Holloway? Did a marriage certificate alter the fact that Ann Kennett was bigamously wed? No doubt about it, John Holloway had that in common with the late monarch - to each of them, marriage certificates were no more than bits of paper.

Holloway?

I try to weigh him up, this bigamist.

I study his portrait.

Is it the face of a Bible-spouting true believer? Can I see him as a member of the Tract Society devoting his boyhood years to delivering pamphlets of deep religious significance? Does he look like a one-time Sunday school teacher?

Is this a young fellow just gone to the bad, a petty thief, capable of stealing a watch and chain from a drunken man sleeping it off in a barn? Does he look the type to convince a servant-girl to let him guard her trunk and then, when her back is turned, to steal the quarter's wages she has inside? Can I see such duplicity in his features?

John William Holloway in Horsham Gaol
From a painting by J Parez

Has the young man - young, because he will never be old - the marks of courage on his face? He has served in the Blockade Service, has led a rough, dangerous life at sea and on land, combating smugglers. How would he acquit himself in these circumstances?

And the ladies' man, any sign of that? We know about Sarah

Johnson whom he truly loved - or so he said; we know about Sarah Harman too. Then there was Celia Bashford whom he married and Maria Burke whom he did not. There was Sarah Sanders, whose end is such a puzzle. And Ann Kennett, another puzzler, who was with him that awful night in Donkey Row. There was another woman he set up in her own house. He left her before the rent fell due. There was also the girl he tried to seduce in a rowing boat at Brighton. And the prostitutes. And others more innocent for he was on his own account a practised seducer.

A ladies' man, yes, even if he had little love for most of them and not a hint of constancy for any.

But the real question always crops up when I look at John Holloway's portrait. Is this the face of a murderer? Can it be discerned in his features, that cold, murderous quality which he surely had? I just cannot see it.

In fact, I cannot see much in the portrait. Not even the aching fear he must have experienced when it was painted for he knew then, as he sat in Horsham gaol, that in weeks he must surely hang.

Other things are similarly concealed. I cannot judge that he is barely five feet tall. Nor can I tell, even if he cannot spell well, that he writes fluently, convincingly, with style and confidence. In gaol awaiting trial he writes extensively about his life. For a boy of such modest learning opportunities, for a man who has wasted much of his short life, he writes very impressively. Other evidence will suggest that he is a fluent, convincing speaker too. He can persuade people. Especially women. Though not always for several will speak against him, of his violence, of what he himself calls his 'savage nature'.

In the last days of his freedom John Holloway lives in Margaret Street, one of those terraces at right angles to the sea, in ugly contrast to the gracious crescents which look out over the Channel. He is on the edge of a crowded rookery of high-density, low-quality building that lies between St James' Street and Edward Street. Here are workmen's cottages, lodging houses, little workshops, jerry-built tenements, beershops. It is a random world. The Watch is continuously called out to the disturbances here, especially at night, to resolve brawls, domestic upheavals, petty offences. Here, a stroll away from the Royal Pavilion, live unskilled men, hawkers, journeymen, craftsmen, farm labourers, fishermen, out-of-works, drunks, ne'er-do-wells, chancers, women on the game, full or part time. It is a shifting, unsettled population. These streets, courts, alleyways are 'an intolerable nuisance to the town at large' according to Dr Jenks' report to the Poor Law Commissioners a few years later. 'They are the resort of tramps, begging imposters and prostitutes of the lowest description'.

It is a squalid, dark little world, yet only a few hundred yards from the fine new elegant squares and gracious terraces of this ultra-fashionable spa town. They flock here, the noblemen, the landed gentry, the substantial professional classes, the comfortable tradesfolk. They come for the Theatre Royal; for the assembly rooms; for the baths, churches, inns. They come for that wonder of the new age, the Chain Pier; for the reading rooms; the entertainments; for the Pump Room.

A visitor from Milan, Count Pecchio, in a letter home writes:

> 'Houses, food, horses, everything is here even more expensive than in London. But the sky is free from fog and fumes; from October to January Brighton is inhabited only by Dukes and Peers. Here you can see, daily and gratis, a princess of the royal blood, four duchesses, etc. taking their walk.'

The King walks along the Chain Pier, marvelling at the skill of his century. He glories in its construction. It reminds him of 'the most beautiful place in the world - the deck of a ship'.

And below him, on those very days when he promenades along the pier, when he raises his hat and smiles, when he accosts his subjects, when he engages them in conversation - well, below the King on such days, Holloway, discharged now from the Blockade Service, sits in a little boat or among the intricate metal spars, and paints the understructure. But where the King smiles, Holloway broods. Nothing can be further from Holloway's mind than theatre plays, taking the waters, military displays, receptions, balls, the forthcoming coronation. Nor to be truthful does the painter have rural disorder on his mind or pressure from politicians for political reform.

But in the early summer of 1831 Holloway most certainly has grave matters of concern to him.

First, though, consider him when young.

John William Holloway, born in Lewes on 22 May 1806, was taken almost straightaway to live with his grandparents at Litlington for his father was away at the wars and his mother shared her husband's campaigns. Not until 1815 when Napoleon was at last sent packing did the child meet his father. And then, it was in France.

Some time later, with his father now discharged, they all, grandparents, parents and children, lived in Litlington. The returned soldier received 12/- each week from the parish for work was hard to come by and he had an extra 3/- as an army pension. Not riches, but enough to pay a few weekly pence for the boy to learn his letters at the local dame school. Later, he went to Alfriston National School where, aged ten, eleven or so, he was appointed pupil-teacher. In those days young Holloway attended the very active chapel in Alfriston and years later, the minister, the Revd Mr Betts and the senior trustee, Charles Brooker, would recall his good qualities.

At some stage, in about 1818 perhaps, the family moved to Brighton, a growing town, a vibrant place, where an old soldier's family might have better opportunities.

In the early years at Brighton, the chapel, first the Baptist and then the Wesleyan, played a significant part in the youngster's life. Every waking hour on a Sunday, if we are to believe his account, was devoted to prayer, to scripture reading, to chapel going. And time on weekdays too was found for these activities.

So then what happened?

Holloway claimed that he fell in with bad company; that he started to drink, to leave off regular chapel attendance, to become an unreliable worker. Nevertheless, this descent into idleness, unreliability and then petty dishonesties is sudden. It is unaccountable, this fall. It is so out of character with a home-loving, church-going young man. Have we missed something? Was it always there in him, a crude quality, a vicious, callous streak? Did the dangerous man always lurk there?

At Brighton Races, Holloway met a servant girl, Celia Bashford. How she loved him, he said.

'She was never happy but when with me; but as I did not love her, I only laughed at her folly; and, to tell the

5

truth, I was ashamed to be seen with her until after dark and then to get out of the town and on the hills as soon as possible.'

Holloway was seventeen or eighteen when he met Celia; she was eleven years older. Perhaps the age disparity was an embarrassment. Or was it her appearance? Was it the disproportionately large head? Was it her diminutive stature for she was only 4'3"? Was it her long arms, her hands turned outwards 'like the paws of a mole'?

Yet whatever his feelings, Holloway did not break off the association. Over the next year or two he went out with her although he left Brighton for some months when he went off to try to find a ship but failed. On the way home, he did some begging; he stole a watch and chain from a sleeping drunk in the barn they were sharing for the night. He seems to have learnt at this time to take lodgings and to leave without paying, carrying with him whatever he fancied.

Where now is the Sunday School teacher, the young man at prayer?

Then he returned to Brighton and it is possible that he left and came back on other occasions. He was no longer settled. But he met Sarah Johnson whom he sincerely loved or so he was later to say. His friends, he claimed, persuaded him to give her up. Why they did so he never explained. Would there not have been greater pressure, even if unspoken, for him to finish with Celia? Sarah Harman was another girl he spent time with but neither did that last. He gave her up. Or so he says. Might it not be possible that these young women gave him up? Might it not be possible that even then they saw something in the boy's nature which made them uneasy?

And then, Celia, a thirty year old woman now, revealed that she was pregnant. And Holloway, nineteen, resisted marriage and found himself clapped in Lewes Gaol by the Overseers of Ardingly, Celia's home parish. Would he guarantee to support her? They wanted no further responsibility for bastards. He could either agree to look after her and the prospective infant or he could stay where he was.

After five weeks Holloway relented, was released, went to Ardingly and was married. Then the parish officers told him they would not have him stay there. Had he work? No. Well then, he could take himself and his wife to his own parish. Let them have the keeping of them. Why should Ardingly be lumbered with an out-of-work husband and wife and child?

Resentful, Holloway and Celia returned to Brighton. For some days they were in the workhouse in separate wings. Then, he found a temporary gardening job in Dysart Street. The newly-weds, with furniture bought by Holloway's father, moved into lodgings, first in George Street, then in Nelson Street, in that part of Brighton where Celia would spend the rest of her days and where he would live intermittently.

He had learnt now, Holloway said, that Celia had not been made pregnant by him but by someone called Edward Goldsmith. She always denied this and perhaps this is yet one of several instances of Holloway seeking to justify his actions, his callousness, his own unfaithfulness.

The child was stillborn and Holloway would brood on his ill-fortune, his marriage to what he would come to call 'a repellent object'. This marriage had all been for nothing.

Holloway next found work with a bookseller, William Nute, a Wesleyan who was never to desert Holloway, who stayed with him even to his last moments. Nute would always testify to the young man's good work. Good or no, however, Holloway gave up the job though whether he had other work to go to is uncertain. It seems unlikely for the couple were soon in desperate need.

When Maria Burke, a fifteen year old, came to share their lodgings, matters, we are told, came to 'a very improper pass'. But then things always would for Holloway had a taste for the ladies. And even if Maria at least eased the problems with the rent, the Holloways continued hard up.

In desperation, and this was only a few weeks after her miscarriage, Celia wrote to her brother for money. Half way between Henfield and Brighton, Holloway met his brother-in-law who gave him fifteen shillings. It would tide them over. Or it would have done had not Holloway spent most of it at a pub on the way home.

Was this the trouble? Was it drink?

Whatever it was, Celia's brother was at the house within days. There was a fearful row. It ended up with Celia going home to Ardingly with her brother, taking the furniture with her. For this, the brother gave Holloway two sovereigns. He was to brood on that too. After all, his father had given them the furniture. How he resented Celia's family. Years later, on trial for his life, he would accuse them and the parish officers of Ardingly for setting him off on the road to the scaffold.

With Celia gone, there was an interlude with Maria Burke who stayed on in the bare rooms until Holloway was persuaded by his parents to give her up. These relationships with women were often frail. Just as he had been persuaded to give up Sarah Johnson, so with Maria Burke.

For a while, free of domestic encumbrances, Holloway went to sea. He signed on for one trip on a collier but did not re-sign, claiming that the ship's master was against him. When he tried to enlist on a man o'war, he was ordered off the ship by the captain who considered him unsuitable. His reservations are nowhere stated but what was it that prevented Holloway being taken on in a fleet which accommodated both the best and worst of men?

Returning to Brighton, for a while he lived with his parents. While working as a builder for the brewer George Wigney he was accused of some dishonesty or other - again there are no details - and either left or was dismissed.

Celia, by now, had returned to Brighton and Holloway took up with her once more, finding them new lodgings in Albion Street and then in Circus Street. There were arguments; he was drunk at times; he manhandled her; there were other women. Holloway was at loggerheads with one of his landlords who took Celia's side against him. He had never loved her: he was coming to hate her.

Yet Celia does not seem to have been so hateful a woman. The evidence certainly speaks in her favour. One of her former employers, a woman with whom she was in service, wrote:

> 'I was very sorry when she married John Holloway as I was afraid he would not use her well; and it is well known that he frequently left her and took up with others. She would frequently say to me she would not mind dying under his hands for she always thought she should.'

James Simmonds, her last landlord, described her as 'a quiet, harmless woman' and his wife 'always had a high opinion of her chastity'. Celia's sister, Catherine, stated, 'He treated my sister very ill. He almost starved her to death'. The only adverse opinions on Celia were advanced by Celia's husband.

In September 1827, with Celia again pregnant, Holloway, still only twenty-one, left home once more to join the Blockade Service. He was in the Service for four years until its disbandment. He served at sea and in watch towers on shore. It was hard, demanding work and naval discipline was severe. Yet, Holloway seems not to have complained. Rather, the impression comes over when he writes of this period that for him this was an enjoyable time. He makes no mention of encounters with smugglers either at sea or on land but doubtless there were some. For example, he was stationed at the watch house at Jury's Gut, east of Camber. This was a favourite landing spot for smugglers and it was here, in 1829, that the last convoy of the notorious Aldington Gang landed and went openly through Lydd, cheered on by people in the street. It is inconceivable that Holloway was not involved in the highly dangerous struggles with such smuggling parties.

At sea, he was aboard a lugger, 'The Badger', and the brig 'Adder', based at Rye. He worked principally as a painter but he also carried out watch duties.

Some time during his stay in the Rye area he met Sarah Sanders.

'I acknowledge that I did promise to marry her soon after our acquaintance began,' Holloway confesses. He had joined the Service under the name of Goldsmith, his mother's surname and incidentally the surname of the man whom he had accused of Celia's first pregnancy. Certainly his adoption of this name would have made for fewer complications had he committed bigamy with Sarah Sanders. But it was not to be. He discovered that 'she was a girl of very bad character'.

She was inconstant it appears. She had another lover. Such infidelity on the part of a woman - on the part of *his* woman - was insupportable.

'We quarrelled and I was heard to threaten her by a woman of the name of Frost. From that time to the present I have never, to my knowledge, seen her.'

And then he continues:

9

'But it happened, after I was gone from Rye, that a young woman was found dead, apparently washed on shore; and I think it was said when found that she had a rope around her neck; but the particulars I do not know as I was not there at the time. I only know what I heard when I returned; and I believe it was likewise said that she was in the family way, and her earrings torn out of her ears; and in many other respects her body had the marks of violence on it.'

I think it was said .... the particulars I do not know .... I only know what I heard .... I believe it was likewise said ......

'Now after this young woman was found,' Holloway goes on, 'it was observed that Sarah Sanders was missing and that the last time she was seen was in my company and that she was likewise in the family way. It was immediately said that the young woman that was found was the said Sarah Sanders. On hearing of this, Mrs Frost went forward and stated that she heard me threaten her very much and that she believed the deceased was the said Sarah Sanders and that she had not been seen since. On this evidence a warrant issued out for my apprehension.'

Holloway was questioned on the matter but his captain is alleged to have given him his alibi. Perhaps, as the captain is understood to have said, Holloway was away at sea when the girl was alleged to have been murdered. Just a few years later, however, doubts were to be expressed about the thoroughness of the investigation.

So was it sheer bad luck that Holloway should have been implicated in this murder? Was the girl washed up on shore the one that he had threatened? Or was Sarah Sanders alive and well and now away from the district?

'God is my witness,' says Holloway. 'I am innocent of that murder.'

And at this distance in time, we must allow him his innocence.

.... But the threats; the strangulation with a cord; the pregnant woman ....

10

Ann Kennett on trial in 1831

There is no way of knowing exactly when the paths of John Holloway and Ann Kennett first crossed. But like Sarah Sanders, she lived in Rye. For some or other reason, Holloway was doing a favour for the wife of an officer also stationed at Jury's Gut watch house. She had asked him to call at a dressmaker's shop in Rye to collect a garment for her. Holloway must have seemed, on the surface at any rate, the kind of man who could be approached by a lady and entrusted with a message. It was at the dressmaker's that he met Ann, then aged about twenty. She already had two illegitimate children though where she and they were living at the time is not known.

What developed was a real love affair, Holloway tells us. When he came off watch, at whatever hour, he would walk the five miles to Rye to see Ann, presumably to sleep with her and then return to duty at the watch house.

How are we to view Ann Kennett?

Are we to see her as 'very sociable and comfortable ... a harmless and inoffensive woman ... a good sort of woman'? She was described by different witnesses in these terms.

Or just the opposite? 'The Atrocious Murder' contains Holloway's confessions and an account of his life but these are wrapped within a commentary. Ann Kennett is described by the commentator as 'one of the most finished fiends which the history of the female sex can produce'.

Readers must reach their own conclusions on Ann Kennett.

The most significant event which can be dated in the uncertain chronology of Holloway's career is recorded in the Rye Parish Records.

'William Goldsmith of the parish of Winchelsea, bachelor, and Ann Kennett of this parish, spinster, were married by licence, in the parish church of Rye, the 16th day of March, 1830, by J.S. Myers, officiating minister.'

Just as with Celia four years' earlier the Overseers had called on Holloway. A woman of the parish was pregnant. He was the father. Could he maintain her? Would he maintain her?

Certainly he ought to have been able to do so. He was still in the Blockade Service and being regularly paid.

But this being the case, why did Ann Kennett think it necessary to ask the parish officers to remind Holloway of his responsibility? When it came to it, did he at first resist marrying her? Did he have second thoughts? He does seem to have loved Ann Kennett more seriously than the other women in his life. Was it perhaps that bigamy no longer seemed such a good idea?

If he was resisting bigamy it was not because of any finer

feelings for Celia. He was to admit that 'he did not care what became of her'. Their one year old daughter, Agnes, their second child, had died; Celia was destitute, living on the parish, earning a few pence selling pins and cotton from a tray. It was not any concern of his.

Early the following year, Holloway was discharged from the Blockade Service. He and Ann Kennett - she had miscarried - went to Brighton seeking work. Almost straightaway Celia knew of their arrival. She was not concerned to have her husband back. Whilst she knew he and Ann were living together under the name of Goldsmith, she was not aware of their bigamous marriage. This was of little importance to Celia. She had become accustomed to being without him. But she did need money.

Fearing that Celia would have the parish Overseers chasing him for cash, Holloway left the town, taking Ann Kennett with him.

In his account of this period, Holloway says that he now became a coiner, boasting of being able to pass sovereigns and shillings and of being generally successful at it. He bought a cloak and was accepted - in some circles - as a gentleman. He and Ann worked their way along the coast, spending time at Eastbourne and Hastings and enjoying some extravagant living. Returning to Brighton, Holloway recounts how he picked up a woman and put her in comfortable lodgings with a servant. He passed her off as his wife and promised to marry her. Then, just as suddenly, he left her.

It was no joke, he writes. It was the woman's own fault. Women should be on the alert; they should look out for themselves; they should not allow themselves to be taken in. Men will always make fools of women if they can.

Then the coining stopped; the money ran short; he was desperate for work. There is no explanation of this change in his fortunes. Perhaps Holloway had exaggerated his success. If he was so good at it, why did he not continue with his money-making game? Certainly he was proud of this achievement. But is it true?

In the late spring of 1831, the couple found lodgings at 7 Margaret Street. It was a poor terraced house, the best he could afford from the wages of his new employment as a painter working for the Royal Chain Pier Company. The house was conveniently situated for his work. But only months earlier he had quit Brighton because of Celia. Now he was back living only a short walk from her lodgings at 4 Cavendish Place where she shared accommodation with her sister and brother-in-law.

As might be expected, as soon as she learnt of his presence, she applied in early May to the Overseers of the Poor. She wanted maintenance to ease her desperate poverty.

How Holloway felt about this is obvious. Though he cannot have been surprised, he was reluctant to pay and angry too. Why should he pay for a woman he did not love, a woman he had been tricked into marrying, a woman who with her family had always caused him difficulties?

It is not possible to say when Ann Kennett learnt of her true status or of her so-called husband's real name. Perhaps she knew of the circumstances before leaving Rye. Whatever the truth of the matter, she must have known the answer to these questions by mid-June when Holloway and Celia met the parish officers. He agreed to pay 2s per week maintenance.

Then heavy rain over several days caused Holloway to be laid off work. Within three weeks he could afford to send her only 1s 6d and later, he could manage only a shilling.

He and Celia argued over this.

Ann Kennett was usually the bearer of the money. She was later to say that on occasion she pawned clothing to make up the deficit. Holloway related how she was always kind to Celia, taking her butter, tea, eggs, bacon. But then, why not take her the few pence she was owed if they could afford the food?

Amelia Simmonds, at whose house Celia lodged, explained in court how Ann Kennett had brought 1s on 4 July:

"'I have brought it from your husband."

Celia replied, "Is that all you have brought me?" She appeared angry and said, "I have nothing to eat. What am I to do with 1s? I will go to the Overseer to know which John is to keep - his wife or his whore." She took the poker and struck Kennett twice. Kennett took hold of her and said "You are too little to hit, but mind, you shall suffer for this." Kennett went away very angry. She repeated the words two or three times.'

Holloway went round to 4 Cavendish Place that evening. Why,

he asked Celia, had she gone to the Overseer again? Landlord James Simmonds takes up the story.

'She said, because he had taken her pay off.

He said, "Madam, you think you are going to frighten me but you are mistaken."

He was then so violent that I ordered him out of doors. He went out and then said to Celia, "You damned bitch, you shall suffer for this before many days."'

Another witness was warned by Holloway not to interfere.

'"You don't know as much about me as a great many or you would mind your p's and q's."'

Celia does, however, present us with another unsolved mystery. She was pregnant again. Was Simmonds the father? Holloway had suggested that he was. Had Celia slept with him? There is no reason to believe that she had. After all, at the time of conception she was not living at Cavendish Place. She might not have even known Simmonds. Was there another man? Or had Holloway himself at some stage, late in the previous year, had the opportunity to sleep with her. Whatever the truth, could Celia, deformed, unloved by her husband, impoverished, be blamed if with some other man she had sought comfort or affection?

The argument on 4 July marks the date when Holloway resolved to rid himself of Celia. He began by forbidding her to visit his mother and she seems to have obeyed him in this, not visiting the old woman in the last days of her life. As a consequence of this, when she went missing, Mrs Holloway assumed that she had left Brighton for London which was the tale that Holloway put about.

If the ex-sailor was to kill her, he needed her away from Cavendish Place. And this is where his plan becomes cumbersome. He planned that Celia should die in another house and for the next week spent time looking for a suitable place to rent. Eventually he found one in North Steine Row - better known as Donkey Row. It was a short distance across the road from The Pavilion. A grocer, Francis Taylor, let it to him for 2/6 a week. And remarkably it was only a hundred yards or so from Cavendish Place.

Incredibly, Celia fell in with her husband's scheme. Only ten days earlier, they had been at loggerheads: by Thursday, 14 July, she was quite prepared to go with him to start a new life together.

Where?

He did not tell her.

Perhaps he intended it to be a surprise; perhaps that is how he passed it off. Holloway must have been at his most persuasive. Over the years he and Celia had argued; he had beaten her; he had taken up with other women; he had left her; he had denied her money; he had threatened her; he had flaunted Ann Kennett in front of her, sending her with the maintenance money. Days before, it had been plain that he not only loved Ann but that he hated Celia. Yet, within the space of days, he had persuaded Celia to leave the lodgings in which she seemed as happy as circumstances allowed; he had persuaded her to go with him, her violent, unreliable husband, to an unknown destination. Did Celia not pause to reflect?

And what about Ann Kennett?

Celia must have asked what was to happen to her. She must have been satisfied with the answer. Had he suggested that he intended to give up Ann?

And did not the Simmonds wonder at the folly of it all? And what about the Bishops, Celia's sister and brother-in-law? Did none of them find the proposals too astonishing to believe? Did they not ask where she was going to live? Did not they have the slightest doubts?

How could any of them have brought themselves to believe what they were hearing? Should a woman, due to have a child within two weeks, be troubled in this way, at this time? Did no one wonder about that?

Were they all equally persuaded by Holloway? Did he really reassure them that they were off to London for a new start?

On 14 July, Holloway called at Cavendish Place. He had come for Celia's clothes which she had put in a trunk. He would also take the bed and mattress. He had found some temporary lodgings, he said. They were going into them prior to leaving for London.

Holloway told Celia that he would come back for her later in the day. She gave him a penny for a half-pint of beer and went off to the bakery to buy him a bread pudding for his dinner. Before leaving the house, he helped himself to sixpence, all she had, in her workbox.

Holloway went off with the trunk, the bed and the mattress to Donkey Row. Perhaps he had already borrowed the wheelbarrow that he needed for later. Ann Kennett was waiting in the house.

We are asked to believe that this was the first time Holloway revealed his intentions to Ann. But for what reason had she gone to Donkey Row? They already had lodgings. Now, Holloway, laden down with Celia's property, explained to Ann Kennett what he planned. But what was her response? She loved Holloway; she recognised Celia as an obstacle as well as a constant drain on their uncertain finances. But murder is another matter. Even if they had earlier spoken in a wishful sort of way of Celia's death; even if they had hypothesised about it, this was reality. We are expected to believe that in the middle of a morning, Holloway informed Ann Kennett that he intended to murder his wife in a few hours' time. Is it believable? It is believable only if Ann Kennett is the fiend that the commentator in Holloway's 'Life' believed her to be.

But suppose her innocent. Suppose her appalled. What then were her possible courses of action? She could have warned Celia; she could have told the parish constable; she could have gone to see the Simmonds or the Bishops; she could have begged friends to intercede, to persuade Holloway of the madness of his plan. Or she might simply have left him. She must have realised where his violent nature was leading them.

Yet all she did was to try to make him change his mind because she feared he might be caught.

Holloway later confessed to frightening her into compliance but even so it is difficult to believe.

Here is Holloway:

'She said I had better not do it for fear of being discovered. I told her I would trust to that if she would assist me; she said, yes, she would.'

It does not seem to have been much of a struggle. Holloway then continues:

'As I had got the clothes, we knew not hardly how to dispose of them.'

17

This is interesting. It proves that the clothes were not taken simply to raise money. They had been got out of the house so that it would appear that Celia had planned to leave, to go to London. Had she disappeared, with the clothes left at Cavendish Place suspicions would have been instantly aroused.

'I said we would pledge some and burn what would not pledge and Kennett took them and I believe pledged them.'

Celia and not the pledge money was more important to him at that time.

Ann Kennett stayed in 11 Donkey Row while Holloway went back to Cavendish Place. Did she have any doubts as she sat in the empty house, bare of furniture, with only Celia's trunk, bed and mattress? Did she dread Holloway's return? She knew what was to be done when he came.

Did Holloway himself with Celia in tow entertain any doubts? As he walked the short distance with her how did he behave? What did he say to her? Did he want to change the plan? Forget it totally?

It does not seem so.

When Holloway and Celia reached the southern end of Donkey Row, he told her to wait whilst he went into the house. She must have thought that strange. He had made some excuse, offered some reason, of course. A friend of his was sharing the house, he said, and he might be asleep. Holloway did not wish to waken him. He would first check, go to the house, see what the man was doing.

So Celia waited in the late afternoon sun, looking up the street at the blank-walled terrace houses, at number 11, the only house with shutters.

Holloway, in the house, instructed Ann Kennett to wait in the cupboard in the corner of the room.

'I then went and called Celia. When she was in the house I shut the door, told her I wanted to wait a little while because my partner lived upstairs and he was in bed and we must wait until he got up and with that pretence I kept her in conversation for some time.'

They went across the brick-floored downstairs room to the open

18

stairway.

> 'I asked her to sit down on the stairs and then on the pretence of kissing her I passed a line around her neck and strangled her.'

So the despised, much abused Celia, only moments before she died, must have come to believe that her husband, so unsatisfactory for the last six years, was at last turning over a new leaf. Poor Celia, deceived to the very end.

And then, surely, a stroke of genius.

Murderer's genius, that is.

For just suppose at some future time, they were no longer lovers, Ann and he. Suppose that for some or other reason she decided to tell what had happened at Donkey Row. There can be no other reason for what occurred next than that Holloway determined to involve Ann Kennett yet more deeply in the crime.

> 'As soon as I passed the line around her neck, I found it was rather more than I could manage,' he says.

Nonsense.

Holloway was a strong enough man, strong enough to murder tiny Celia, the pregnant woman with the mole-like hands.

> 'I called Ann and God knows she assisted me by taking hold of each end of the rope with me and she held the rope with me till the poor girl dropped.'

And these words implicate Ann Kennett, make her equally guilty with her lover.

Holloway continues, giving Ann some Lady Macbeth-like lines.

> 'I held the cord for a time myself and Ann made use of this expression, "Do not let your heart fail you".'

Did Ann Kennett encourage him so? She was supposed to have been presented with the murder plan only hours before. Were those witnesses who spoke highly of her totally wrong? Or was Holloway the only liar and monster?

19

'When I thought she was dead, or nearly dead,' Holloway goes on, 'I dragged her into a cupboard or coal hole under the stairs and under the stairs there is some nails. I did not remove the cord but took an over-handed knot and I made the ends fast to the nails so that she was hanging by the neck.'

It was all the work of minutes. Celia had come away from Cavendish Place not half an hour earlier. She must have been in 11 Donkey Row no more than five minutes before she was strung up in the cupboard.

And next? Well, she could not be left there.

'I proposed then cutting her. Ann Kennett told me to wait until the blood settled.'

So the body was left and they started a fire in the grate, burning some of those items of clothing, bonnets and the like, which were unlikely to be pawned. But whilst this went on, they knew that other work awaited them.

On the following morning, they returned to Donkey Row. There was the mattress they had brought and Holloway poured the chaff filling out of it. He needed the cover.

Then he set to.

'I cut off the head first and I think the arms I carried with the head. Ann Kennett was present. I never went to the house to do anything with the body but what I took Ann Kennett with me. And the day that I brought the head and the other parts away, she was to walk behind me to see if any blood came through. The first attempt we made would not do because the blood came through the ticken [sic]. Ann told me of it and we went back and put it into a little box and then into the ticken.'

The head and limbs which Holloway severed on the brick floor of the downstairs room were taken back to Margaret Street. Ann had previously asked one of her neighbours not to lock the back door explaining that Holloway would be out late, smuggling. When that night they returned together with the box with its awful

20

contents in the mattress cover, they let themselves into the back area. They dropped the contents of the box into the common privy.

A woodcut published after Holloway's execution

But there was still work to do.

The rest of Celia Holloway was still at the house in Donkey Row. It had been placed in the trunk which had held Celia's clothes.

Ann had washed the floor.

Washed it and washed it.

The next day, she went to the pawnshop, pledging three gowns and an apron, giving her name as Ann Goldsmith. When she returned later with other articles she gave the name Brown and said that she lived in Carlton Row.

That night, Holloway and Ann returned to Donkey Row. They carried out the trunk, placing it on the wheelbarrow. He led the way pushing the barrow, she following with a pick and shovel.

Up the hill they went with their grim cargo, beyond the bounds of the town and into Preston Village. Here they passed the Hare and Hounds, silent and dark. Well into the country now, yet only about a mile from Donkey Row, they turned up the footpath leading to New England Farm and then crossed a field to a copse near Lovers Walk, that track on most other occasions so aptly named.

Though Holloway was to recall it as a beautiful night, it was too dark to dig a grave. They put the trunk, the pick and shovel under some bushes, returning home with the barrow.

As soon as it was light the following morning they were back at the intended burial place. It was difficult to dig much of a hole because of the tangle of tree roots. In the end, confessing himself defeated, Holloway stopped digging. The torso was flung out of the box and into the shallow hole. Immediately it was covered with soil. Then the wooden trunk was broken up and the pieces scattered about. That evening Holloway and his mistress returned to retrieve the pick and shovel which had been left hidden under bushes.

Some days later Holloway went back to the site to check the grave. On two other occasions, Ann Kennett visited. There seemed to be no cause for worry.

Yet they must have been anxious. People in Donkey Row had seen them coming and going. One of the occupants, Holloway later said, called out to him and 'abused me very much, told me that was not my wife I was with'. Those living there must have asked themselves why there had been so much activity for two or three days and why this had suddenly stopped.

Others too must have raised questions. Those in Cavendish Square and Margaret Street must certainly have been puzzled. But when questions were raised with Holloway, he informed them that Celia had found work as a chamber maid in London. She had taken all her clothes with her, he told people. She'd put them in a trunk and taken them with her.

How he explained events to the Simmonds and the Bishops is not clear. He must have had a convincing story for mystified as they must have been at the apparent change of plan, none of them thought to take the trouble to call the constable.

Did Holloway and Ann Kennett feel safe?

The guilty couple moved away from Margaret Street at the end of the week following the murder. But they went only as far as lodgings in neighbouring High Street. In the end, they were among the same people, walking the same streets. And the whole tacky business, the unsatisfactory story with all its loose ends about Celia's move, must have haunted them.

So did they feel safe?

And how did Ann Kennett feel when one evening she met her lover with a prostitute on his arm? When she remonstrated with him, he hit her, cutting her forehead. This was only weeks after that fearful event which one might have thought had bound them for life.

It was the heavy rain only a week or so after the hasty burial that shifted the earth. Just the smallest piece of red cotton appeared on the surface. And if a man chanced along, he might well entertain suspicions about new turned earth and a piece of cotton. He might well wonder about what lay beneath.

Certainly on 25 July the labourer Daniel Mascall was curious enough to tell his friends about what he had seen up there in the copse at Lovers Walk. The earth looked to have been newly dug and the piece of thread he had pulled had produced a length of cloth.

Mascall and his friend, Abraham Gillom, went up after some days and considered the soil. When they poked it with a stick it smelt strong and unpleasant. When they went back to Preston they told their families and other friends but never said a word to anybody in authority.

On Saturday morning, 13 August, Gillom, his mother and sister, and a Mrs Sherlock decided to make an expedition to inspect the plot that Mascall had first seen three weeks earlier. After consideration, they decided to call in the parish constable, William Elphick.

He brought a spade with him. He turned up a bundle of clothing tied with string. When he opened it, he found the

23

headless, limbless torso with a male foetus protruding from it.

In the course of the day the news spread as Celia's remains were removed to a nearby barn. They attracted thousands, some of whom, for payment, were allowed sight of the body. Others zealously fulfilled their civic duty by searching the fields and hedgerows for the missing head and limbs or any other exciting souvenirs. The very branches of the tree which overhung the grave were carried off.

By evening, it was news in Brighton that a body had been found.

Old Mrs Holloway heard about it. She had already had a dream that something dreadful had happened to Celia. Now she sought out her son. He, too, had heard what people were saying. But he was able to reassure his mother. Celia had gone to London.

He would go to the constable, however, and give whatever help he could. He would tell them about her, that she had found work in London. He had seen her off as far as Preston. She intended to catch the first coach to London. They were regular enough. Over forty coaches a day went from Brighton to London. She intended catching one of those. He had, by the way, given her £9; she had saved £1 of her own money.

For a time there might have been some hope. Word was out that the body was that of the daughter of a staymaker who lived in Edward Street. She had gone to Brighton Races and had disappeared. Why, even her father had viewed the corpse and had sworn it was his daughter lying there. He had recognised her by the stays she was wearing.

But if they placed any hopes on the corpse of the staymaker's daughter, Holloway and Ann Kennett were to be disappointed. Late on the Saturday evening, on the very day that Gillom and the others had visited the site where Celia lay, the lovers were placed under arrest.

The following evening, Sunday 14 August, an inquest was held at The Hare and Hounds, that silent pub that the two lovers had passed with the wheelbarrow. Outside, a huge crowd jostled, trying to catch a glimpse of the principals and the activities within. Were they able to see, they might have noticed the bookcase which had been placed between Holloway and Ann Kennett to prevent their communicating. And had those outside been able to hear, they might have listened to Catherine Bishop, the dead woman's sister, relate the sad history of Celia's marriage; to Dr Hargreaves telling the coroner's jury that Celia had gone into labour at the time she was being done to death; to Amelia Simmonds identifying the pieces of wood as belonging to the trunk in which Celia's clothes had been removed.

At the end the jury returned a verdict of Wilful Murder against Holloway. He was sent to Horsham Gaol. Ann Kennett was remanded for further questioning and sent to Lewes House of Correction.

That same evening, Mr Folkard, High Constable of Brighton, and his officers, searching for the dismembered limbs and head, directed their attention to Margaret Street. They searched the rooms occupied by Holloway and Ann. Then the common privy was emptied. Near the bottom were found the stockinged legs, the arms still in their sleeves, and inside the mattress cover, Celia's head.

Small wonder that The Times was to report on 16 August that 'the town of Brighton and for miles around has been thrown into the greatest excitation which was not exceeded by the horrible death of Maria Marten in the Red Barn at Polstead'.

There followed a number of examinations of Holloway at Horsham, of Ann Kennett first at the Sea House Inn in Brighton and later at Lewes.

For a time, Holloway stuck by his story that he had accompanied Celia to Preston from where she intended to catch a coach to London.

Ann, meanwhile, was asked to explain the shattered trunk. Dissatisfied with what they heard, she was remanded by the magistrates for a further examination.

On Saturday, 27 August, Holloway asked to see the Brighton minister, Edward Everard. He was now anxious to take full responsibility for the crime. He wished to confess. In front of three magistrates, and unprompted by questions, he gave a fluent account of all that had occurred.

Holloway admitted that he had strangled his wife and cut up her body. He blamed her family for their unkindness to him. Had they been more friendly, he would have resumed living with her. Instead, because they had done all in their power to make him wretched, and because Celia herself had done her utmost to destroy his peace of mind, he had been driven to the act, for he had been determined on revenge.

This was a highly charged, emotional outpouring. 'His cries, yes, almost his shrieks for the mercy of God upon his soul, were most humble, most appalling,' Everard said about this first confession.

Ann Kennett underwent another examination on Monday 28 August, when her neighbours from Margaret Street spoke of seeing her and Holloway carrying a parcel late at night. She was remanded for a further week. At her final examination, a witness spoke of the argument between Ann and the murdered woman. She had said, 'I won't hit you, Celia. You are too little for me, particularly in the state you are in.' She had followed that up, however, with repeated threats.

All the same, several had spoken of Kennett as an inoffensive woman. Ann Lever, her landlady, thought her harmless and sympathised with her saying she was ill-treated by Holloway.

'I only interfered in the quarrels,' Mrs Lever said, 'for fear she might get from [Holloway] some unlucky blow.'

Ann Kennett was bound over to appear at the Winter Assizes.

Early in September, Holloway wrote several letters to his mother, acknowledging his guilt, assuring her of his repentance and of his confident expectation of escaping hell-fire. These letters, and indeed most of his extensive writings at this time, throb with religious enthusiasm. They contain sermons on the avoidance of sin, dire warnings of what befalls transgressors and throughout they are studded with Biblical references and quotations. He was constantly reading, too, and praying.

Was he sincere?

Whether or not he was, he was certainly impressive. Everard wrote:

'It cannot indeed be denied that the mind of Holloway, formed as it was by the professors of Christ, is not one of an ordinary stamp, and that, in fact, it displays an energy possessed by few.'

26

Energy, certainly.

But can we believe this rapid conversion? Is the practised seducer to be believed when he counsels women who, he says, encompass their own ruin? Perhaps he does now believe. Perhaps he is now converted.

Holloway next asked if he might see Ann Kennett. He wanted a meeting arranged so that he could persuade her to reveal all she knew.

Ann was conveyed from Lewes to Horsham Gaol. When they met in front of the magistrates, her first words were, 'Oh, John, to what have you brought me?'

But 'in language most energetic' and 'calling on God, before whom he was so shortly to appear, to aid him in his persuasions, to induce her compliance,' he begged her to tell the magistrates the full tale.

At this, Ann rounded on him, hitting the table violently and calling him 'deceptive wretch', 'villain', and 'blackguard'. Did he not know she was innocent, she asked. The devil had possessed Holloway, she declared, and he was trying to ruin her.

Holloway swore that he loved her but, 'if she did not disclose all she knew, he could not appease the wrath of Heaven; how could he hope for forgiveness of his crimes if he left the world in ignorance of the facts which were yet undiscovered and he again urged her to reveal all she knew.'

But the woman continued to abuse him, to deny there was anything to tell.

What was Holloway after? Are there signs here of incipient religious mania? Or was he simply a religious humbug, the ultimate betrayer? Ann Kennett's view was that he did not wish her to escape to marry someone else.

Or was there really something else to reveal?

The matter was never very enthusiastically pursued but a hammer had been found among Ann Kennett's possessions. It had been borrowed from a neighbour and never returned. It had been washed and scraped clean.

Washed of blood?

Perhaps so, for it was among some bloody rags found in the High Street lodgings.

Had Holloway told the full truth about the murder? Did Ann help him despatch Celia? He said that she too had pulled the cord round the neck. But supposing the real truth was that when he had called Ann to help him, she had come out of the cupboard with a hammer. There had been a bruise on Celia's forehead.

But if so, why had not Holloway told that version of the murder?

Unanswerable.

And despite Holloway's pleading that she should tell all she knew, the hammer was never mentioned at the Horsham meeting.

And so they parted. They would not meet again until the trial: they would never again exchange words. The magistrates, for their part, received a poor impression of Kennett. Where Holloway had been calm, she had been violent and rowdy. Not that this was evidence of her guilt. But the magistrates were uneasy, too, about the cool way in which Ann Kennett, only minutes before in a rage with her lover, now coolly asked for her own clothing. She asked not to stay at Horsham but to be taken back to Lewes even though she complained about the Keeper of the House of Correction. Of course, these were not unreasonable requests. For their part the magistrates might simply have been of the opinion that anyone in Ann Kennett's situation - and particularly a woman - should not feel able to make such requests.

Holloway's third confession is a curious mangled document in which he tried to confuse matters. There were two Ann Kennetts he wrote. One of them, but not the one in custody, had helped him murder Celia. The authorities needed to find her and release the Ann Kennett now held in Lewes.

In a day or so, Holloway was writing a letter to the High Constable of Brighton full of concern, repeating Ann's request for her clothing. He also bequeathed her all his belongings.

Nearer to the trial, however, Holloway confirmed in a letter to the magistrates that he now stood by his second confession. He wished to bring, 'none but the guilty to justice but since that I have let that love which I have toward her overrule me and I have, out of pity to her life, tried to throw a veil over the real truth, and as far as I could, screen her from justice. This, I am sorry to say, I have done against the powerful workings of my own conscience but cannot any longer contain myself till the real truth is known. My first and second statement is truth.'

He had thereby condemned Ann Kennett.

So what may we believe?

Did Ann Kennett play a greater part in the murder than we have been told?

At Lewes Assizes on 15 December, 1831, before Mr Justice Patteson, John Holloway faced a charge of murder and Ann Kennett was accused as an accessory of aiding, abetting, comforting and assisting him during the commission of the crime.

At times, Ann was tearful; she fainted; she had to be physically supported; she had at one point to be taken out of the court room.

But Holloway, dressed for the occasion in his sailor's clothing, was ferocious.

On his way into court, a small boy, a bystander, had pointed the prisoner out. He could recognise Holloway, he said. Before his escorts could restrain him, Holloway had hit the boy in the face. It was in that ferocious mood that the court met him.

At the outset he insisted that the charges be read a second time.

'I don't understand a word of it,' he said.

He was aggressive, arrogant, challenging, angry.

When it was repeated, he shouted fiercely, 'I am not guilty of all that that paper charges me with.'

Asked how he pleaded, he replied 'with utmost ferocity' that he was not guilty until the case was proved against him.

What a contrast with the zealous, contrite, prayerful man of recent months. In prison, he had written much of his youth when 'against all the temptations of Satan, I, through grace, kept pressing forward with my face Zionward'. Perhaps a paragon was expected in the courtroom at Lewes.

Not so.

Whenever he had the opportunity, he challenged witnesses, refuting their statements, in a hostile fashion.

But it was all too strong, the case against him. He railed against those responsible for his being there, Celia's family and the Overseers at Ardingly who all those years ago had tricked him into marrying. It was they who had brought him to this pass. They were the villains.

At least, he told the court that Ann Kennett was innocent, that whatever part she had played was because he had forced her. In any event, she was dismissed early in the proceedings. The Judge opined that she was not guilty of murder. It was and is astonishing.

The trial lasted a day. Holloway was found guilty.

New charges of being an accessory after the fact were to be brought against Ann Kennett.

Holloway was hanged at Horsham on Friday, 21 December. In the morning he took the sacrament. On the scaffold he went down on his knees to pray. He kissed the Bible, exhorted the crowd of two thousand to mend their ways. And left this life.

After the body had hung a little while, a labourer from Cowfold climbed up onto the staging. He had an unsightly wen on his forehead. Could he have it touched by the dead man, he asked. He could. Holloway's wrists were untied for this. And a handkerchief was placed on the still sweaty chest of the dead man for the applicant. Dead man's sweat, a sovereign cure.

Two women seeking similar favours of the hangman were sent packing.

Holloway's corpse was returned by coach to Brighton. For twenty-four hours it was exhibited at the Town Hall where 23,000 men, women and children, came to wonder at it. The body was then removed to the hospital for dissection.

In March Ann Kennett, a mother now, appeared at Lewes Assizes, her baby in her arms. She was charged as an accessory after the fact.

The proceedings were brief.

She was discharged. She had convinced a judge and jury of her innocence.

She has not been traced by this researcher.

She was not likely to be found in those turbulent, bawling streets where she and Holloway had set up house for some few months. Even that grim place could never accept so stained a woman, for Holloway's crime was her crime. Ann Kennett must have sought some other haven, some other identity.

In that other Brighton, only a few hundred yards away from where Celia, Holloway and Ann Kennett had lived, all went on as before - the banquets; the grand levées; the balls; fireworks lit up night skies; the coronation was celebrated even while John

Holloway and Ann Kennett waited in prison; the aristocracy regularly came and went; the York and Albion hotels flourished; Mrs Fitzherbert, restored to royal favour and a regular visitor to The Pavilion, was given permission for her retainers to wear royal livery; Her Grace the Duchess of Argyll and Lady Agnes Paget took up residence in the Old Steine; a Miss Smith, a clever little girl, delighted audiences with her dulcet tones and at Tuppen's Library Miss Corle's voice was thought to be much improved on the previous season; King William, amiable, chatty, continued to tread the Chain Pier. The world went on: life went on.

Nevertheless, some things linger in the mind. Odd snatches of speech, passages from letters. Sometimes, trying to work out what kind of man this Holloway was, one remembers the admission he made to his mother. It was as well he had been caught, he told her, for had he not been stopped, he might have gone to greater lengths. And we think yet again about Sarah Sanders.

In a letter to William Nute, that loyal former employer, Holloway expressed the hope that he would meet Celia in glory. Is that really what he hoped and expected?

On another occasion, when he admitted to having beaten Ann Kennett black and blue, to having torn the hair out of her head, he had confessed that he had done this 'for what reason I do not know. It was my savage nature.'

Holloway's 'savage nature', what else might it have been responsible for?

SOURCES

Sue Farrant, 'Georgian Brighton, 1740-1820', University of Sussex, 1980

John Holloway, 'An Authentic and Faithful History of the Atrocious Murder of Celia Holloway ... published by his own Desire for the Benefit of Young People', 1832

G S Jenks, 'On the Sanitary Condition of Brighton 1840', (see 'The Chadwick Report'), BPP, 1842

Clifford Musgrave, 'Life in Brighton', Hallewell, 1981

Sussex Advertiser
The Times